A View
from
HEAVEN

Chief Apostle Dr. Paris Miller

ISBN 978-1-63961-875-0 (paperback)
ISBN 978-1-63961-876-7 (digital)

Christian Faith Publishing, Inc.
832 Park Avenue
Meadville, PA 16335
www.christianfaithpublishing.com

Printed in the United States of America

Contents

Foreword

Apostle Paris Miller is a person with real, tangible leadership credibility in all areas of every profession she has engaged in by evident proof of her communion with the Holy Spirit and her years of ministerial service, excellence, and sacrifice. Leaders think differently than nonleaders, and their mindset and behaviors show this dichotomy. The average person doesn't spend time reflecting on lessons learned from their daily rigor and how to make tomorrow better. Leaders are reflective people who don't just look at the good; they also evaluate the not so good, the mistakes they made, and what they can do to be more productive, even and essentially in the lives of others. A leader who stands out when it comes to this intangible quality is Apostle Paris Miller.

Apostle Paris's mind is quick and agile and defies gravity, meaning she does not let it descend and dwell in the low places of hopelessness, despair, or condemnation. As a thought leader, she is always thinking over the purest form of revelation, the highest good for her fellow citizens, and ideas to elevate the people of God and those who are connected and will be to her. Her mind and spirit have mastered a strategic engagement of the heart of God through worship to feel His thoughts, and her heart solemnly embraces the mind of Christ to communicate revelation in an unprecedented way to show the unique ability of God through His anointed ones.

She would be the first to let you know that you are valuable in who you are and what you think about matters. Apostle Paris uses thought-probing questions by the Spirit, which opens and tunes into your spirit to help you develop as a Christian and grow as a person. Questions such as what makes you unique? What captures your imagination? What do you dream about? What makes you sad or angry? What learning from the past and this present experience have you gathered? What do you want to change? Where are you going and want to go in life? What is God constantly saying to you? These are the kinds of things that leaders like Apostle Paris provoke people to think about.

There is nothing wrong with being a hard worker and a good laborer; the world needs them. However, the world also needs great thinkers and provokers. Apostle Paris Miller is a great thinker, a master of spiritual provocation, and a great leader.

To understand these thoughts, I propose on a deeper level that everyone must look at their own thinking. The thoughts everyone thinks toward a situation influence the circumstances on an unconscious or spiritual level, if you will, toward that particular situation in some unique form. Better thoughts may not change present circumstances, but they can present a better person and may prevent future negative events. The things I ponder, dwell on, and allow into my belief system become my actuality and reality. Dwelling and pondering on the negative replays it and patterns it in my mind, allowing it to return as frequently as it wants to in rotation. Dwelling and meditating on the positive reiterates powerful encouragement to my life and produces the fruit of those thoughts.

The moment I met and embraced Apostle Paris Miller and her teachings, I began to think differently, and my life changed. She encouraged me to lift my mind to a higher level of thinking (God thoughts) and my understanding (God ways). I instantly entered into a higher level of living regardless of the outward presence. The moment I returned to my old lower way of thinking, my life returned to the old lower way of behavior and living.

"There are no limitations except those you acknowledge. Whatever you can (mentally) conceive and (spiritually) believe, you can achieve," said Napoleon Hill. Apostle Paris Miller embodies the previous statement, and she is a breath of fresh air to those who are struggling to breathe and in need of freedom from a life of bondage. The Most High God is a God of decency and order, not ironclad rules and regulations. She has embraced the mantra and mantle of Moses that heralds, "Let my people go, that they may worship the true and living God!"

She has been blessed with the innate power to unleash your wings and cause you to soar to heights you were told that were not possible for you and release you to fly without binding you to her emotional or personal attachment. You are struggling because you need to be celebrated and loved unconditionally for who you are and the things you have accomplished and overcome, as she would say in a soft-spoken manner that vibrates like thunder through the core of your being! She walks the earth humbly among us as a servant unsung, loved but not given her due benevolence according to my view.

However, in the heavens, Apostle Paris Miller is a champion of faith who has opened doors and sacrificed much for The Most High God and His son Christ Jesus's sons and daughters' voices to resound in the earth. She is a Queen of queens and a Lord of lords, and may her legacy and labor of love in the trenches, trials, and turbulence of ministry be rewarded in her lifetime and afterward. He honors and pays obeisance to the queen and woman of unrivaled faith and passion for God and His people, the esteemed Apostle Paris Miller.

—Apostle John Solomon

Introduction

Why am I here revealing some of my life's experiences with YOU? Why do this now? What is the purpose of unveiling or exposure now? Why the name of this publication? The name changed many times. When I thought that I had the final name, the Holy Spirit changed it again.

Simply put, why not now! Some people do care what the Holy Spirit says and reveals to me and to others with similar encounters. Someone needs to know and someone needs to know now! What I have discovered is that people are on the verge of suicide and abandoning their dreams and visions and need to be encouraged through some other means. Some should know that *who they are hearing from and what they are seeing* is from Jehovah God! You are not crazy! Yes, we are peculiar and odd; however, there are many of us in this world. Because He shared with me, He will, or has done it for and with YOU! YOU are not alone in your experiences nor in YOUR hearing or seeing. YOU need your own confirmation! This is it! I call YOU forth...come forth NOW, YOU, yes YOU...in Jesus's name!

Life is so precious and is worthy to be lived! Most people are not living, yet barely existing in the small sphere that they are in. Some only know how to walk down the street to the corner store or go next door. They have never ventured outside their neighborhood, let alone driving inner city where they reside. Some never owned a vehicle! Some have never journeyed to the north or west sides of their residential city.

Some don't know the voice of Jehovah God or that He talks to or communes with us. I was inspired by many who prophesied me to write books. Many seasoned apostles, chief apostles, and prophets spoke these words to me. The activation came through Sister Myra Omofoma one Sunday afternoon while visiting one of my spiritual daughters, Apostle LaTanga Renfroe. As we sat around speaking and eventually prophesying to each other, I asked Myra, "*What is Holy Spirit saying to you?*"

She said, "*I don't know!*"

I moved on, and we continued to fellowship. All of a sudden, Myra blurted out, "*When are you going to write those books?*"

I became very cognizant that the Holy Spirit was speaking to me through her. Myra continued, "You should have written two books by the end of 2020." This month was October 2020! I completed this writing prior to the end of December 2020.

Therefore, people of God, my time is now! That self-same night, I was awakened early the next morning with titles and the first chapter course of this script. He first uttered the title *Heavens Thunder!* He—Holy Spirit—has also given me more book titles including this one, *A View from Heaven*. As they say, "The rest is history!"

Everything written here is true...**ALL** of it! I lived ALL this and more. This is just a foretaste. These *visions* are real for those that believe and for those that do not believe also.

Journey with me!

Beginning the Journey: Set Up

Part 1
Get Up

*A*s I recall these days of moving forward, I smile when thinking of how Jehovah God set me up for *my next*. While having *the need* to temporarily live with family because of homelessness, I was invited to dwell with a friend of the family, who became one of my dearest friends. She was necessary for my life and taught me so much. She was amazing! After living there for some time, Holy Spirit began to speak to me there. I was awakened from my sleep early one morning to the words, "*Get up!*" My sleep wouldn't release me from the bed. Again, the voice said, "*Get up!*"

I looked around my room to see if my roommate had called me. No, she hadn't! Louder became the voice. "*GET UP!*"

Slowly I sat up in bed and became more alert. Then I knew that it was the Holy Spirit speaking to me as I was becoming aware of spiritual things. He then said, *"Get a sheet of paper and a pen."*

There was paper and a pen near me. With pen and paper in hand, His next words were, *"Make a list!"*

Okay, here I am hearing these words. He further spoke, *"Document this list with two columns. On the left side place the item I will speak to you; in the right column draw a line by each item.* My hearing was very good! Picturing His instructions and being well-trained as a typing instructor, I was given the vision of what this was to look like.

He spoke, itemizing from room to room. I wrote! He uttered:

Bathroom:	Bath towels	_____
	Shower curtains	_____
	Bathroom window curtains	_____
	(I knew most apartments don't have windows in the bathroom.)	
	Bathroom rugs	_____
	Toiletries	_____
Kitchen:	Dish towels	_____
	Dish drain	_____
	Silverware	_____
	Place setting (dishes)	_____
	Glasses	_____
	Can opener	_____
	Microwave	_____
	Pots and pans	_____
	Refrigerator	_____
	(I knew most apartments have refrigerators)	

	Food, etc.	_____
	Mop and broom	_____
Dining Room:		
	Table, chairs	_____
	Rug	_____
Bedroom:	Beds	_____
	Linens (queen-size)	_____
	Rugs	_____
	Nightstands	_____
	Chairs	_____
	Drapes	_____
	Comforters	_____
	Lamps	_____
Living Room:		
	Sofa and chair	_____
	End tables and coffee table	_____
	Rug	_____
	Lamps	_____
	Drapes	_____
	TVs	

Jehovah instructed me to type this list up and take it to work and ask coworkers that He would reveal to me for help from this list. He said, "*If you tell them that you have relocated after giving all your paraphernalia away, they will help you. Ask them to write their name on the line for the item they wish to donate. Need I tell you that everything on the list was supplied?*"

My prayer partner said, "You have everything on the list but clocks. I will get you some clocks!"

Wow! My new place was fully furnished. Everyone fulfilled their vow without delay.

Do you get it? I was set up by the One Who is omniscient. The One Who knows our past, our today, and our tomorrows. He made sure that I was awakened and wrote as He articulated. Am I glad that He spoke and I obeyed...you, too, right? I received more from this list than I had given away prior to leaving Atlanta to journey to middle Georgia!

Part 2
Church Mother

There were prerequisites for the upcoming blessings! I was tested. There was this dear **church mother** whom I called every morning upon arrival to work. I always arrived thirty minutes early to work. She encouraged me, and I encouraged her. She prayed for me, and I prayed for her. This particular morning, she asked, "*Baby, now I tell you I will pay you back. I promise you I will pay you back by the first of the month.*"

I asked, "Mother, what is it?"

She continued to confess, "*I will pay you back.*"

I relented and said, "I know that you will, Mother. How may I help you?"

She said, "I need $45."

I said, "Okay, when do you need it?"

She continued, "By Monday."

"Is Saturday good for me to come by with the money?" I said.

"Yes," she said! Today was Wednesday.

In the meantime, a friend of the family knew that I was ready to move from my present residence with a roommate to my own place. She called and said, "*Hey, I cleaned up this office building in the historic district, and they have an apartment above their office that they are renting. It is gorgeous. It is a two-bedroom apartment with a huge bathroom the size of a bedroom with many windows.*"

"When will you be there?" I asked.

She said, "Saturday morning, about 10:00 a.m."

"May I come by then?"

"Yes, of course," she said.

For me, this "Yes" was with excitement! There was something about this "Yes" that pleased me and filled me with enthusiasm and expectation.

Saturday morning came. I journeyed over to the location. She was there and greeted me on the outside. I loved the historic neighborhood and the quietness of the area. We entered the building through the main office of the business. As we walked through, she identified each part. Then we entered a hallway. On the right side was a downstairs one-bedroom apartment occupied by a ninety-two-year-old retired, renowned pianist!

She said, "The vacant one is upstairs!"

I looked up and ascended up the eighteen flights of steps! They were beautiful antique mahogany wood steps. As she opened the heavy wood door, I was astonished at its splendor and peace. We toured each room. I loved it!

"It is mine," I said to her.

She smiled and said, *"Okay, I will tell the landlord that I know you and that you are interested."*

Oh my God! What is going on here, Father Jehovah? What are You up to? Yes!

Well, I left there excited and encouraged! It was Saturday and time to take my church mother her $45. As I exited the expressway to her place, I made a left turn. To the left was a Kroger grocery store.

Holy Spirit said, *"You know that she likes collard greens. Go on in there and get her some greens."*

Yes, sir, I will! Entering Kroger, I saw the statuesque big leaves of the collard greens. My excitement to get these for her activated Yahweh to continue to check my obedience to Him. He said, "*Well, what if she doesn't have any boiling meat to cook the greens with?*"

Okay, here I am going to get the boiling meat. I knew what she liked because we talked every morning. He then said, "*What if she doesn't have any meal for corn bread?*"

I got the meal and the buttermilk, even sugar. Again, He said, "*What kind of meat will she eat with the greens?*"

I went for turkey wings then for sweet potatoes then for sausage...on to bacon, then eggs...then bread, milk, mayo, lunch meat, etc. He said lastly, "*You know that she likes peach sodas!*"

I begin to scan the store to purchase much more than the peach sodas before He challenged me again. Here I am with a buggy full of groceries for this lady that I loved so much. She had a need. I wept with joy at the opportunity to be a blessing to her. She certainly was to me. You may not understand this, but even my vehicle was overcome with excitement. It seemed to drive better and lighter. As I migrated closer and closer to her efficient apartment, I called to say that I was almost there. "Okay, baby," she would often say.

Upon arrival, I knocked at her door with groceries in both hands. She opened the door, smiling. In my overjoyed obedient voice, I said, "I am here. I made it!"

She smiled with few teeth in her mouth. Mother looked down at my hands, put her hands over her mouth, and asked, "What is this?"

I could hardly stand it! "Girlfriend," I said. "This is for you!"

She returned her hands to her mouth again and said, "*For me!*"

Excitedly I responded, "*Yes, ALL for you!*"

"But I can't pay you back for these groceries."

I said, "You don't have to. This is from God."

"Oh my" was her response.

Remember, I can hardly breathe because of my obedience and excitement to our Father to help her. I was more exhilarated than she was! I proceeded to the tiny kitchenette to put the groceries away. As I opened the tiny, half-pint refrigerator, there was hardly anything in it. Each purchased item had its own place in the refrigerator. It was all a perfect fit. Her refrigerator was full! She was as excited as I was!

We talked and then I gave her the $45 that she had asked for. All I could hear from Mother was, "*Now, baby, I am going to pay you back!*"

"No, Mother, I will not accept any money from you. Just continue to pray for your baby girl," I uttered!

Again, she insisted on paying me back. Throughout her lifetime, I did not accept any money from her. We were friends until her demise years later.

Part 3
The Vacant Apartment

After all this weekend's excitement, Monday came, and it was now time to call the landlord regarding **the (my) vacant apartment**. His secretary shared that he was scheduled to return to the office on Thursday. Prior to his arrival, I had left several messages with this secretary of my interest in the vacancy. Thursday came and I had the opportunity to speak with him. I identified myself as his new tenant. He thought that was so funny and laughed! He said, "*Well, we will see!*"

I asked, "When may I come to sign my lease?"

Again, he thought that was funny! I don't know about all that he uttered! "Mr. Refrigerator," I asked. "May we talk in person?"

Saturday was confirmed as the day we were to meet. As I entered his presence on Saturday, I was greeted by this tall handsome Caucasian businessman. He was humble with a handsome smile. We talked at length. This was the beginning of him sharing his life with me. Our conversation was lengthy and consuming until he finally rose and said, "*Oh, I am supposed to show you the apartment.*"

I corrected him and said, "*My apartment!*" He looked at me with glee and shook his head in awe.

As we traveled up the eighteen steps, he began to share with me these things. He said, "I have had three people inquiring to look at the apartment and their lives didn't align with my criteria."

As he looked me in my eyes and stated, "I only rent to Mercer University College students. One was in a wheelchair and couldn't get up the steps. Another couldn't move in until next semester. The third one had personal mental issues, and this would have been too much of a risk for me."

"*That is because it is mine, Mr. Refrigerator!*"

Again, he shook his head and said, "*Ms. Miller, you are something else, but... I like you!*"

That big *but...*! I was almost there! I started my verbal launch of truth to him with, "*Mr. Refrigerator, I will pay my rent before time, I am a professional businesswoman, I don't have parties, and I am a clean-cut, quiet, for-real, church-going woman with only a very few visitors! I will be the best and most memorable tenant that you will ever have...even be your confidant.*" We had already talked for what seemed like hours!

He said, "*Okay, I will give you a try!*"

I grabbed him, pulled him close, and hugged and thanked him! I was so thankful. Even though he was handsome, my hug was not an Eros hug. It was an embrace to God for opening this door for me to begin my new life of independence in this new city and a "*You won't regret this*" to him.

As we toured each room, he told me of his plans to paint every room. Then, he thought for a moment, looked at me, and said, "*If you paint it, I will buy the paint, the throw cloths, cleaning solutions, and reduce your rent.*" What?

"Okay." Then I remembered that I didn't know how to paint and told him.

He said, "That is okay. I will teach you how to paint!" People, this is real!

With paint in his hands, we met on the assigned day for the painting lesson. He ended up doing most of the painting as we laughed and talked. With help, I finally finished and moved in! He and I had the best landlord-and-tenant relationship. Some days as I arrived home after work, he would be waiting for me and would call me into his office to talk and confide for long periods. Most days I became his personal counselor and therapist. Some advice he would take and some he wouldn't. He was a grown businessman. This was his life.

I made sure that I was available because he was troubled and I was thankful to him. We never lost our professional relationship and respect for each other. I lived there for the duration of his lifetime—five years! He died and I and the downstairs tenant, Em, were given three months to vacate the premises by the family. What a blessing he was to me and Em. I was never late with my rent payments nor did I break my living covenant with him. I kept my vow to him, therefore, to Jehovah God!

Yahweh set me up for this new life by challenging my obedience to His command to help Mother, my landlord, Mr. Refrigerator, and Em.

Part 4
Em

*E*m, as I called her, whose name was **Margaret**, was the sweetest neighbor a girl could have. Immediately the landlord, Mr. Refrigerator, introduced us. She had lived there for some years prior to my arrival. Our relationship was not mother-daughter yet friend-to-friend. It really grew and matured. I was family to her and she to me! We became besties!

Em was ninety-two years young and was a world traveler who was once a renowned pianist. She had all the memorabilia to prove it. She still drove her own car throughout the United States. She would say, "Paris, I am going to Virginia. I will return in a month."

One month later, she returned home alone. She always invited me to travel with her. She would say, "You don't have to worry about a thing."

I was a working girl who was jump-starting my new career in a new city, so I declined. As she journeyed on the road, she told me that she would drive fifty-five miles per hour for four hours, get out and have lunch, get back in the car, and drive for two more hours then get a hotel room and start over the next day until she reached her destination. She charted her path and learned various languages for the journey that she was taking. Em had French and Spanish language books that she learned prior to her visits abroad. I am so thankful that Jehovah kept her safe and well so that I could share my life with her, and she her life with me.

It was either she or the landlord who would stop me as I entered the front door of our building after work each day. Before I could get upstairs to my place, her door in the hallway would be open as I arrived home. She would say, "*Come on in and have a cocktail to settle your nerves!*"

Her glass was always full of something, and there was always a pot on the stove. Most of the stuff in the pot I could never identify! However, I knew that she was a healthy eater. The spirited cocktails would slur her language, and she would curse about everything. We laughed about everything. I loved this woman, and she loved me.

As our relationship progressed, she would paint a picture with words of her life's journey—Carnegie Hall, opera houses, plays, Argentina, Paris—written memoirs that she showed me!

"Em," I said. "What are you going to do with your documented memoirs?"

"Give them to my namesake to publish," she resounded!

There was this gorgeous hot-yellow antique chair in her apartment she purchased abroad that I wanted. She said, "Okay, let me check with my granddaughter to see if she wants it."

She told me that her granddaughter was there for the chair the very next day! We had been neighbors and friends for about two years, and I had never seen her granddaughter, her namesake. I didn't see namesake when she came for the chair the next day!

Shortly after this, at the age of ninety-five, my friend Em became ill and was hospitalized. Every day after work, I visited my friend. On one of these visits, I met her namesake. We talked and she thanked me for being such a good friend to her namesake grandmother. On another afternoon's visit to the hospital, Em's namesake said to me, "Paris, the doctor said that grandmother can't drive her car anymore, so here are the keys to her car."

She threw Em's keys to me and said, "Her car is yours! I will sign the title over to you within the month." This she did! Again, this is real!

Every morning prior to this incident as I left for work, I would look at Em's little car parked outside and say, "*How can she get in that little car. No one can fit in there!*"

Em was five feet or so, she said. She was really four feet ten inches. I am five feet twelve inches. You do know that this car was perfect for me to drive. I drove it for five years, and my six-foot-five brother drove it afterward.

My friend died shortly after her hospitalization and rehab. I wave at her grave as I pass the cemetery where she is buried. I still miss her and the landlord today. They were so necessary toward my matriculation in life. I still testify of their necessity on my life's journey.

Part 5
Dr. Wonderful

At this juncture in my life, after I relocated from Atlanta to middle Georgia, it was difficult to find full-time employment. Working with temporary services was my means of almost surviving.

Because I was unable to secure permanent employment for two years, I was blessed to find a full-time, long-term assignment through a temporary agency. I worked on this temporary assignment for nine months as a secretary. At this assignment, one of my constituencies was so evil! She would say things like, "Nobody likes you here. You think that you are going to get my job, but you are not. I have been here for a long time. Just because you have a BS degree doesn't mean that you are smart!" The tone in which she spoke was so demonically deep!

I withstood this turmoil in order to reestablish my lifestyle. Satan was using her and Jehovah God was strengthening me. Even though I reported her twice, the powers that be didn't believe me. She had job tenure, a fake smile, and a satanic personality. Now I know that the powers that be didn't understand spiritual things or evil things either, so they couldn't help me.

Having been at this establishment for almost nine months, on one particular workday, one of the vice presidents called me at this office and introduced herself to me. She said, "Ms. Miller, I will have a vacancy for an administrative assistant. I know of your works, and I would like for you to apply for it."

I thanked her and acknowledged, "*Okay!*"

The evil coworker was listening and said, "If I were you, I wouldn't apply for that job because she has had eight administrative assistants in eight years. No one can work with her. She is awful!"

Well, I didn't apply. Two days later, the vice president called me again. She said, "Ms. Miller, I called HR, and they don't have your application yet."

With regret, I apologized to her and said that I would apply. That same demon overheard my conversation again with the VP and repeated, "I told you that no one can work with her. Her current AA is leaving because of this."

I didn't apply. Two more days went by. The VP called again a third time and said, "Ms. Miller, I am sending you an application."

I said, "Okay, **Dr. Wonderful!**"

Shortly after my conversation with Dr. Wonderful the same day, the dean came to my desk and said, "Ms. Miller, we can no longer keep you. Our temporary contract with you will end this Friday!" It was Wednesday! He continued, "You have worked well with us!" Us... I worked well with you but not that demon.

Nevertheless, I went immediately to HR and applied for the vacant AA position. The interview took place the following day, and I was hired on the spot by the VP and started to work the following Monday.

I found out that it was true that the vice president had eight AAs in eight years by speaking with the AA who was leaving. However, I worked with her for four years. I overheard the university president's conversation with Dr. Wonderful in her office door. He said, "Oh, you have someone now that you can work with!"

She chuckled and smiled. Dr. Wonderful brought me fresh flower bouquets every Monday morning. She left after my fourth year, and I remained with the university for one more year. What a setup!

The Encounter

It all began in an intercessory prayer room across the sanctuary in the church that I was a member of. You see, I was the coordinator of the Intercessory Prayer Ministry. Holy Spirit instructed me to assign intercessors during every church service to pray as the pastor preached. My obedient self put pen to paper and followed His instructions by making assignments for the intercessors. I made schedules for the *gap standers*. They were to be on post during each of the three Sunday services.

On this particular Sunday morning at the 9:00 a.m. service, I had an **encounter** as never before. As Sister Diane and I were fervently praying through this fellowship service, I was taken out of my physical body from the prayer room in the Spirit into the sanctuary. I watched as Holy Spirit was hovering above the congregation. I continually watched everything that was going on from above. As I spiritually looked down on the congregation, He—Holy Spirit—traveled from the back of the sanctuary high above the congregation.

Holy Spirit started to, what I call, *search the crowd.* I guesstimate for about five minutes or so, I watched as He spiritually traveled, moving from the rear of the congregation to the front, left to right, slowly searching and spying out the crowd. From the back of the sanctuary, I was attentive as He slowly gravitated to the front. This is the best way that I know how to describe this encounter. Suddenly, He swooped down and landed into a person sitting on the second pew in the middle section of the sanctuary.

The church was full; as usual, every pew was filled. Then my Spirit returned me from the sanctuary to the intercessory prayer room. I asked Sister Diane, who was on post with me, "Did you see that? I mean what just happened?" Of course, in my excitement to share with her, she was not aware of the things that I hurriedly described to her of my experience across the prayer room in the sanctuary.

I continued to share this encounter with others as I was led to by Holy Spirit. This impacted every fiber of my being. I knew what I saw and what had occurred but couldn't understand it. What did this mean? Why did I see this from a high place? Why did Jehovah search out the sanctuary to find someone? For what purpose? He searched from the back of the sanctuary to the front, shifting from left to right until He found what or who He was looking for. Why?

Several people, Christians and nonbelievers, tried to interpret this vision. Finally, my adjutant explained, "Apostle, that was you that Holy Spirit swooped down into! Don't you remember that is where you always sat in church every Sunday?"

She further stated, "*He was placing Himself into you!*"

Jehovah help me; I passed out, as we call it. "I was slain in the Spirit with these Words!"

This interpretation caused me to put on skates for our Father. Ever since then, I have been hearing and seeing through His eyes. This life of living for Him has taken me on many spiritual journeys like the one just mentioned above.

As I think of it, it really didn't begin with this vision. It all began approximately in the 1980s.

While I lived in Atlanta, Georgia, I began hearing the words, *One Voice-One Voice*! Over a period of years, I was overtaken by these words. As well, many times the voices, as I called them at this time, would crowd me with information. I was disobedient then so I avoided what was spoken or whispered to me.

"Obedience is really better than sacrifice, and submission is better than offering the fat or rams" (1 Samuel 15:22). *Obedience* is a powerful weapon that stems from love, reverence, and trust in God. *Sacrifice* says that I am willing to give it all up for You, Jehovah God. I didn't understand these words! Why was I being challenged with these persistent promptings of One Voice-One Voice?

In the meantime, I continued to live my flamboyant life in Atlanta until my lack of understanding and my disobedience to not seek further these promptings were snatched away from me.

My disobedience to these promptings caused me to be challenged with a lawsuit because my name was similar to someone else's name. I had to seek the counsel of a public defender. This matriculated over a period of three years. I knew, during these years, that I couldn't relent as my attorney continued to tell me my options. He would say, "Well, Ms. Miller, the district attorney says if you plead guilty, you will only have to spend one year in prison and five years on probation."

I asked, "Will I be able to vote when released?" Silly me!

"No," he uttered. Then I responded to him, "No. I do not accept this plea as I am not guilty of what they accuse me of. Maybe of other stuff but not that!"

He returned to me approximately four more times with reduced pleas from the district attorney. Finally, I said to Mr. Telephone, my public defender, "If you come to me one more time with offers from Mr. Nobody—the district attorney—I will go to him personally and represent myself. No more deals! I am not guilty of this!"

Well, this last time, Mr. Telephone called me to say, "The district attorney has dropped all charges against you. Congratulations, Ms. Miller!" This case was closed, and my records were exonerated!

People of God, press for your innocence. Stay the course when you are right!

One Voice-One Voice

Recalling the **One Voice-One Voice** promptings, I now know the purpose! These prophetic words were continuously uttered to me while I lived in Atlanta. I had no clue as to their meaning during that season of my life.

During my transition to middle Georgia, after many tumultuous encounters, I joined the church that my sister was a member of. The pastor was young and anointed to teach and preach the gospels. I gleaned so much from him. I've yet to refer him as my spiritual father, and he is not aware of my attachment to him.

While living with my roommate, Holy Spirit returned to the words, "*One Voice-One Voice!*"

Finally, I asked, "What is One Voice?"

He said, "One Voice Apostolic Ministries International Inc."

"Ministry who?" I countered.

He said, "You. You are to lead One Voice Apostolic Ministries International, Inc."

I countered, "*But I am just growing and getting the opportunity to learn spiritual things.*"

He said, "*You are my leader, and you are to lead this ministry.*"

Who, me? No!

My first thought was, *Okay, this will be a prayer ministry.* I was familiar with this because I currently served in this capacity. I then began researching and searching protocols, legalities, goals, objectives, mission statements, and visions for *One Voice Apostolic Ministries International, Inc.* The first thing I was told was to secure the name with the State of Georgia. I did so and followed their rules and regulations. There was no other ministry with this name. Thank You, Jesus! Jehovah knew this.

After serving with the old church for ten years, Holy Spirit dictated to me a resignation letter from this church. One evening as I was watching television, He said, "Get up and go to the computer."

I did and He began to dictate my resignation letter from that church. He stated, "If you can give two weeks' notice on a job, then you can give two weeks' notice in My house!"

The following Monday, I called the church for an appointment with the pastor to submit my letter of resignation. All week I was unable to secure an appointment. Monday of the second week, I called and was able to connect with the assistant pastor. I entered her office and gave her a copy of the letter and asked that she give the original to the pastor. She questioned me to no end after reading it.

"What are you going to do?" she asked.

I replied, "I already have a ministry. I have had it for two years."

"What is the name of your ministry?" she inquired.

"One Voice Apostolic Ministries International, Inc."

She further questioned, "Who is going to cover you?"

"Holy Spirit will until further notice because He gave it to me." I exited her office after about fifteen minutes of interrogation with her. Respect the office people!

On Tuesday the next day, as I entered the church for my last weekly intercessory prayer gathering there, I was met by the pastor. He was apologetic that I couldn't connect with him the prior week. As well, he stressed his regret at me leaving and complimented me on my service with the church. I informed the intercessory team of my departure as well that selfsame night.

Five days later, my last Sunday, upon arrival at church, as usual, I arrived thirty minutes early to pray around and over the sanctuary as well as to anoint the pews. My usual practice each Sunday was to get the microphones and pray aloud after anointing the pews so that order and focus could remain in God's house.

As I was praying, there was a tap on my right shoulder. There were about eight of us up front praying and agreeing. I continued to pray. The tap returned. I looked behind me to respond to the tap. The person stated in my ear, "Assistant Pastor (AP) says 'to shut it down!'"

I looked into her eyes and said, "Excuse me!"

She repeated, "Assistant Pastor says to shut it down."

I then said into the mic, "In Jesus's name, amen," and proceeded to my chair. The intercessors up front looked at me. I gestured for them to sit also. As I sat down, someone asked, "What happened?" I told her.

She responded, "I know that we are not going to the other location."

My response was, "*I must complete my course here.*"

It is not complete until I leave the other location.

She said, "The AP will call there and tell them not to let you pray there."

"That is her prerogative," I said. "My duty is to complete the course here with no regret of my call."

As we arrived early at the second location, I proceeded to anoint the pews and pray silently. She and I then sat down for service. The technology guru brought the microphone to me, and I prayed aloud. My course was complete there.

The Birthing Room

About eight years ago, I was taken in the Spirit outside myself into a labor and delivery room in a hospital. I watched high above as the mother was in the birthing position with her feet in the stirrups. I saw all the staff assisting with her birthing experience. All of a sudden, as the head begin to push out of the birth canal, there appeared two deep red hands. These two hands were in position at the tip of the vagina to receive this new child into the world. These red hands touched and claimed the child and children as they enter earth.

Since this vision, it has been interpreted to me that these were the hands of Satan claiming each *new child* as they enter earth. The progression of society's ills is such that because of this immediate claiming of babies' lives by Satan, there is much mental illness, more infirmities, much disrespect, and diseases in the world now. Thirty years ago, it was not known for anyone to have cholesterol problems, no AL diseases, no lupus, or shingles; Alzheimer's was not as prevalent or pronounced as it is today. The devil has spewed his evil poison throughout the earth in the lives of the newborns. There are so many babies now with cancer that has never been previously diagnosed; not just in America, but throughout the world. In the devil's evil eyes, what better time to get humans than when they are born?

In years past, when I was in high school, there may have been one person in a classroom that was slow, but not mentally deranged or manic depressive as now. Now children are severely disabled to the point of suicidal death. This evil spirit enters through the children into the home and transfers and infuses the family, the home, the school, the neighborhood, the job, and the church. Pastors and leaders are not equipped to deal with mental disorders because of the magnitude of evil spirits infiltrating the earth now. If there are no intercessors to stand in the gap or to raise up the hedge, this spirit multiplies. Where are you, intercessors? Called saints, we must use the authority and power given to us by Jehovah to combat the tactics of the devil. Do you know who you are! Hear from heaven, strategize, and pray that these red hands are bound and destroyed in Jesus's name.

I have seen people whose leg was turned backward. Knee and foot were in the back of the body; babies born with red skin as if it was raw. All these things are the result of the devil's red hands afflicting babies as they enter the world, even with cancer.

Those of you that are reading this book, please pray over and anoint your pregnant loved ones before they get to the delivery room. Anoint the babies and rededicate them back to Jehovah God when they leave the hospital or after they arrive home. Lift these babies up to Jehovah God and reverse the curse that the enemy placed on them in the delivery room. As well, assist me in praying to annihilate the hands of the devil and to pray for the children that have been affected by these red hands.

A View in Heaven

On another occasion, I had an out-of-body experience where I was looking into an area that was full of dirty, dusty, tumultuous activity and destruction. I watched and knew that this was a war between demons and angelic host beings. I knew this!

The land was desolate and dry. It appeared to be an area that was not visible to us on earth. The demons appeared to be an ashy, dusty, translucent, gray color in their silhouetted form. The angelic hosts appeared brightened, pure yet indescribable. My knowing said, "This isn't a good fight!"

I saw an intermingling of what we call overturning *fist fighting* as in the old cartoons. The turbulence was such that one could hardly tell who would win. I was in this place of view for some time, watching the warring!

The next day, I was taken in the spirit realm back to the same place and the same spot. The area was clear. The dust had settled, and no one and nothing was there. I asked, "Father Jehovah, why did You return me here today. I see nothing?"

He said to let the people know that the true saints *win!* He further stated, "On yesterday, I brought you here to see what was going on behind the scenes so that My people will know that I am always interceding on their behalf."

On yesterday He stated, "Satan had released his demons to distribute a portion of the coronavirus on the earth. I sent my angelic host to annihilate and destroy what his demons were about to release to earth. Some of My children would have been affected with COVID-19 had it been released."

The Holy Spirit continued, "You do know that My children, My remnant, My ecclesia, is targeted by Satan. This was meant for My followers, My disciples, My apostles, My prophets, My pastors, My evangelist, My teachers, My children, My sons and daughters! He comes to kill, steal, and destroy those that are Mine.

"I am your chief intercessor! I need for you to share this with others—that I did come. That YOU would have life and have it fully! Even if you don't want a whole life, I want it for you! There will be those who won't believe this, but tell the few that will. Just as I sent My angels to win the COVID-19 battle on yesterday where they destroyed the work of the devil, I still win battles for those that are Mine. Abide in Me!"

John 15:4 states, "*Abide in Me, and I in you. As the branch cannot bear fruit of itself, unless it abides in the vine, neither can you, unless you abide in Me.*"

The Dinosaur Man

The vision seemed to be so real. I was frightened by the vision! What sort of thing is this? Looking on from afar, I saw this thing that appeared to be a man yet a dinosaur. It had the head of a man but the long neck, the feet, the body, and tail of a dinosaur. It was about twenty feet tall with a tail that was a thick fifteen feet in diameter that slowly followed its path. It resided in a desert of nothing but dryness.

There was so much dry, dusty sand that the sand moved and jumped out of the way when this thing walked. I knew that other smaller creatures were hiding from its rule. I could tell that twigs wouldn't grow because of this fear of it; they didn't want to reproduce because they knew the fate of new growth. I, too, could tell that everything in its midst understood who it was and hid and gave it room to move around. As it lifted its left leg and foot, the ground did a high jump; the few dry twigs afar off bowed down to it as it took its freedom on this desolate terrain.

As I watched, my thinking was, *Where is this place? How far removed away from people does this thing live?* It occupied its territory. It was on full alert and guard and took liberties to move around to make sure the dust, the twigs, the other smaller creatures, and even the ground knew who it was. I never saw the smaller creatures but knew they were there hiding. It maintained its position of prominence in this region.

Even today, Holy Spirit wants us to know of the existence of such demonic beings—their size and the rule they have been given by the devil over certain providences. It was as if this sphere of range is somewhere not visible by humans, yet controlled by the devil.

Pray, saints, pray!

Territorial Buddha

Driving on the way to work early one morning, I was quickened to look up. As I looked up, I saw this humongous thing that looked like what we call a buddha. It was perched in the air with its legs crossed under its body, overlooking this particular area of the city. I stopped my car and gazed at this thing. I knew that it was guarding its assignment as it turned north, south, east, and west to follow the devil's instructions.

Holy Spirit said, "This is the territorial demon assigned by Satan to this part of the city. It does its job exceptionally well! It never leaves its post and watches over every family, every job, every gang, every church, every marriage, every business, and every building on this side of town. It will get punished by Satan if it is not obedient to its father—the devil."

It came from hell and knows the pain and eternal torment that goes on there, so it dares not disobey its master. As this demon watches over this region, it STOPS goodness and kindness if we allow it to. It inflicts DIVISION in churches, marriages, families, coworkers, and schools if we allow it to. It CLOSES down businesses if we allow it to. It infuses filth into food products of restaurants and homes. Territorial spirits are as real as is Satan.

The prince of Persia mentioned in Daniel 10 was pretty powerful because the angelic host that came to Daniel tells him that this mysterious prince had been resisting him for twenty-one days. These territorial demons are no weaklings!

Please know that Holy Spirit told me that "*Satan and his demons can inflict thoughts into our mind, yet they don't know what we are thinking.*" They want to know, so they do this! They are limited in this regard. These spirits MUST BE BOUND! Residents in these areas must corporately repent, guard their territory, bind these demons, and pray!

California Cliff

Years ago, I was granted spiritual access to look upon hillside mansions and estates crumbling into the sea on the California coastline. As I watched, the earth gave way; some dwellings tilted backward toward the water and slowly fell into the sea.

The entire ground and houses dissolved and disappeared into the water. There was no trace of land or dwelling that had previously stood visibly. Would you believe that I heard the screams of the occupants as the crumbling of the soil and the homes tilted and dropped off the face of the earth? If I hadn't seen this spiritually, it would have been hard to believe.

When people go missing and can't be found, could this be a possibility?

These were once drop-dead gorgeous mansions on the edge of the cliffs and waters in California that no longer stand there.

Alligator Warning

In the wee-wee darkness of this Monday morning, on my way to work on this less traveled back road, halfway to work, I looked quickly to my left and saw what appeared to be an alligator watching the road. I dismissed this vision and arrived to work safely.

On Tuesday morning while traveling the same route, again I looked and that same alligator was again on the left side of the road farther down, closer to the school where I was employed. It appeared to be making its way closer to my job. I then became alarmed and began to pray for I knew that this was nothing good.

This was no normal-sized alligator. It sat perched on its high front legs that appeared to be about thirty-five inches off the ground. Its head seemed longer and larger than a full-grown alligator, maybe two and a half feet long. Again, it was on its watch. I shared this vision with my Tuesday night weekly Word study group. As I shared this with Chief Apostle Dr. Davis this night, he stated that he had visited me at the school on Tuesday to bring me some lunch, and there was a man at the school door that would not allow him to enter. This person, he said, told him that I was not there and that he had to leave the premises! He left. This was demonic interference. No one ever monitored the entry doors but me. I remotely allow people to enter the building. After I shared the alligator vision with him, Chief Apostle Dr. Davis clarified that this was a demonic spirit sent against the administration and me so that it could occupy the school, children, families, territory, and the premises.

The following Wednesday, again I journeyed to work. Further down the road, still toward the school, there was this alligator again perched on its front legs with its watchful eye on the road. Upon arrival to work, I was ignited to share these experiences with my principal as he understands spiritual things. As I gracefully entered his office, he closed the door behind me. He knows that I am a professional, faithful employee with eyes to see. As I shared with him these four occurrences over the last three days, he listened attentively! When I finished, he took my hands, and he prayed. I agreed with him.

As I left his office, I shared this with my coworker! She resounded, "I am glad that we have a seer to help us see here at school! *You are our unseen protection. You are here to show us where our enemy is hiding in plain sight. No matter how many came before you or after you, they were unable to see. Your gift, I thank you for it... for being able to see for us...it is like you are hidden in plain sight too!"*

Shortly thereafter, a student entered the office with a windbreaker on with an emblem on it that said, "Hidden in Plain Sight." The emblem was embossed with an alligator figure on it. She excitedly asked, "Ms. Miller, did you see that?"

"No!"

She called the student back and pointed to the emblem with these words on it that she repeated. Then I saw it all and became excited also! We didn't see or recognize this student anymore.

I knew that this alligator vision had been annihilated and could not be fulfilled or activated! What the enemy sent could only manifest on a jacket; not against God Jehovah's people.

Benny Hinn's Angel

While visiting my best friend in Atlanta, one of the purposes of my visit was to go to fellowship at the Phillips Arena with Pastor Benny Hinn and his entourage. I took my best friend's daughter with me. As she and I sat there waiting on Pastor Benny to come out, I made use of this available time of waiting by attempting to lead her to Christ. I asked her, "Do you believe that Jesus is the Son of God?"

She said yes.

Then I asked, "Do you believe that God Jehovah raised Jesus from the dead?"

She responded no!

Then I prayed with her that she would believe one day as this was not the place, nor did I have enough time to share with her.

By this time, the music began and Pastor Benny slowly and gracefully entered the platform. As he entered, he resounded on the microphone his famous words, "*He is here!*"

When he said this, I straightaway saw an illuminated angelic host appear behind Pastor Benny. This angel was about nine feet tall with a flowing pure white robe on.

This robe was billowing and inflating, rising and falling! Part of this angel being's robe was behind Pastor Benny's right-hand side and part of it was visible to me.

It was as if Holy Spirit was saying, "This is my beloved son in whom I am well pleased!" This was an amazing encounter. He allowed me to be an eyewitness to this scene.

The Separation Has Begun

All of a sudden, there I was looking from a distance to hear and view in this special place. I knew this was of God. As I watched, Jehovah God's hand was moving people around from one place into an identified group. He began to identify to me what He was doing.

He showed and verbalized to me three visible groups of people. He explained as He worked, "*The separation has begun!*"

With Him being omniscient, He knew that I questioned, "*What separation?*"

I watched His hands carefully continue to place people in each of the three groups! I thought to myself, *But I thought there were only two groups, the wheat and the tare!*

Holy Spirit continued, "The group of people on the left—Group 1—will never choose Me. They are without hope for everlasting life with Me! Group 1 is lost and doomed for eternal torment in hell! Group 2, that is in the center for now, are straddling the fence. They are neither hot nor cold! They want Me, but they love the world. Time, as you know it today, is on their side. Group 3 on the right is sold out for Me! They won't change.

They have My signet ring on them! The world calls them Holy Rollers. I call them children of the King.

"Group 3 is making their mark in the kingdom! These are those that see Me and hear from Me and do my bidding without fail and at all cost. They are *focus factors* for Me! I can and do send them out into all nations! They are commissioned by Me to do GREAT exploits for My kingdom! They know Me, and I know them. I can depend on them, and they can depend on Me."

After this view and clarity, as quickly as it came, it disappeared, and I was back in this world to share it.

Which group are you in?

The Scarecrow on a Black Horse

Almost immediately following "The Separation has Begun," I was taken to another desolate land. It was a dark place, grayish black in color. The houses, if you call them that, were empty and appeared condemned at the point of falling down. The streets were a dark cobblestone with a few dead plant sprigs up and down the street!

Out of nowhere emerged this black horse with a scarecrow riding it with a black cape on. The horse was moving at jet speed so much so that the cape that the scarecrow had on was caught in the wind behind it. The scarecrow had no teeth, and it knew that it came with a warning to spew poison on the earth. Its eyes were hollow! It rode the horse where its posture was bent because of the urgency of its intent for coming. It was on a mission for his father—the devil! I knew this much! Prepare people of God; fast and pray against this evil mission.

The first thought that I had was, *This reminds me of Paul Revere coming with a warning.* Like the dinosaur man, this view was from another sphere.

I asked various people for their interpretation of this vision. I did receive a few versions.

Dying while Living

A quick view from the left side of the stratospheric heavenly realm is where I was positioned to watch this. While watching, people walked lackadaisically in the middle of the cobblestone street as if the spirit of death was upon them. It was whispered to me by the Holy Spirit that these people had no hope or desire to live. I questioned Jehovah God, "Why?"

He answered, "Because their leaders are not in place to encourage them or teach them or cover them or prophesy to them or pray for them or chastise them or love on them or send them birthday cards and gifts or sow into them."

"They could hardly walk. They stumbled as they slowly moved forward. It appeared as if they did not want to escape death but welcomed it. I knew that they were tired of living and looking for their spiritual benefactor.

"Their assigned leader or covering hasn't received nor accepted their calling for these assigned congregants, therefore, they wandered aimlessly into nothingness hunting for them. Some of these assigned coverings will never believe that they are called to lead My children, so their assigned congregants are *dying while living*!

As I watched them walking weakly and feebly through the street, they strained to walk, stumbling as they wobbled slowly, looking down as if to say, "*Where is my covering, why can't they find me, why aren't they looking for me?*" They thought, *I don't want to die alone. I want my spiritual relationships too! I am ready to be found so that I can live. If you won't come, I won't be able to make it.*

To view and hear this made me feel so sad! Viewing this site put me on a quest to teach regarding *covering!* People of God, P-L-E-A-S-E accept your calling. There are those assigned to you dying aimlessly looking for you. They don't want to give up their life alone. They still anticipate YOU finding them. I knew that these walking dead people were displaced because their assigned leader was displaced and didn't think that they were worthy or equipped to be a leader in the household of faith. All people are assigned a leader whether people believe this or not. Leaders, get up and move toward your chosen stewards so that they can live! These people were giving up because their chosen leader wasn't in place.

The Roped Circle

As I watched from somewhere at a distance, I saw this circle of people, men and women, tightly knit standing in this place, or should I say, in a room of sorts. It seemed as if they were waiting for something. They were stilled, humbled beings, focused on why they were there. I knew this! Suddenly, in the midst or distance were these huge hands that I knew were holy hands.

Immediately, these huge hands took a rope and roped all these people together at the waist, encircling each person at their waist prior to proceeding to the next person. The next person was interlocked and each person thereafter. Afterward, He opened the rope, took one person out, and then closed it again. After taking a person out, He crowned and sealed the person by placing His hand on the top of their head. He then placed each sealed person on His right side of this circle.

Jehovah continued this process of opening and closing the rope, crowning and sealing each person, and placing them on His right side until the rope was empty. It was as if He was sealing them and their place with Him. I saw my face in the rope. I was positioned at His right-hand side.

Thank You, Jesus!

The Chiseling Process Prophesy

Holy Spirit

Early one morning, I was awakened from my bed to the words, **the Chiseling Process**! I knew that I was to document His intent! He revealed to me two groups of people. The group on the "right was the righteous groups." The group on the "left was the unrighteous people."

I thought it strange as I saw God's hand chiseling the silhouette of a righteous person. He chiseled pieces off the shoulders; pieces off the hips and pieces off the feet, etc. Then He revealed to me that the unrighteous people on the left are in constant—nonstop torturous fire and pain. The small chiseling of the righteous ones produces an *original work of art*. Even though the chisel is sharp and produces pain, the finished *work of art* for the righteous ones is well worth Jesus presenting US to His Father, our Father saying, "*L-O-O-K at your handi-work, your workman!*"

Ephesians 2:10 (KJV) states, "**For we are His work-manship, created in Christ Jesus unto good works,**

which God hath before ordained that we should walk in them."

The refiner's fire produces masterpieces! A little discomfort here and there produces a *masterpiece* for God's glory! The love of God WILL NOT keep us in the refiner's fire constantly. The refiner knows how sharp to make the chisels' edge; how long to chisel; who He is chiseling and "how much" the one being chiseled can take. He knows US and knows our future.

Jeremiah 29:11 (NIV) says, "*For I know the plans I have for you," declares the* LORD, *"plans to prosper you and not to harm you, plans to give you hope and a future."* We then become the artist's best work.

He was interpreting to me that when He presents US to His Daddy—our Father Jehovah-Yahweh, He does so with glee and honor. He was rejoicing for us withstanding the process of "the chisel" because WE KNOW that we will turn out as pure gold! "*But He knoweth the way that I take: when He hath tried me, I shall come forth as gold"* (**Job 23:1**). We, too, rejoiced because we withstood the chisel! Good God! The purifier knows.

Jesus willingly allowed the suffering of His flesh to be the occasion for the maturing of His human character, while He walked among us. "*For it became Him* [the Father], *for Whom are all things, and by Whom are all things, in **bringing many sons unto Glory** [US], to make the Captain [Christ Jesus] of their Salvation Perfect through sufferings"* (**Hebrews 2:10; emphasis mine**). Can we do no less but to receive our occasional CHIS-ELING from the Father as His means of perfecting our character? "*Knowing this, that the trying of your faith* worketh patience. *4 But let patience have her perfect work, **that ye may be perfect_and entire**, wanting nothing"* **(James 1:3-4; emphasis mine)**.

Any spiritual growth that ever takes place in our life will always be accompanied by the chiseled trials of life. People of God, *REAP the bounty, the bounty, the harvest for withstanding YOUR chiseling.* Your Father knows and He cares regarding *His finished work—YOU!* The Chiseling Process produces a *perfect body of Christ!* As He chisels an individual, He places us back on the right side in the *body of Christ.*

The Great Day of Awakening Prophesy

"**G**REAT Day of Awakening coming," Holy Spirit whispered!

He continued, "*There is a '**great day of awakening coming**' whereby man won't be able to receive another chance! Time now, as you know it, is being fast tracked for those dragging their feet. I have given you* MUCH TIME *to repent and* STOP *your foolishness. How many warnings do you need? How many prophecies must you hear? Even* NOW, *you know who you are.* STOP PLAYING!"

When will you get right with Me? How many times must I *open the door of forgiveness* and you revisit the old waste places? The sins are ruins for a reason. Ruins are

- deserted places;
- uninhabitable (why do you go there?); and
- desolate, yet some of you CONTINUE to wallow at/in these ruins. **Some are about to be turned over to your choices!**

You do not believe that ALL power in heaven and earth is in My hands...ALL power! I dispense My power ON THE JUST AND THE UNJUST. Good power from Me goes to *the just!* Destructive power goes from Me to the unjust. Which category are you in? (repeat). The door of another chance for some is being closed because YOU, again, you know who you are, you didn't change in time; even with My warnings. Your time is short. Your *length of days* is being shortened with every breath that you breathe! Can you hear Me now? Do you understand the words that I am speaking? Somewhere along the way, some of you forgot. Will you continue to forget, or will you heed these instructions?

I already know who will and who will not. How long must I be with you for you to understand Who I am? How many times must I speak for you to know My voice? The gift of discernment that I gave to you is wavering! Leaders, *hear and heed* this word so that you can share this with your congregations. How long? Not long for some of the disobedient, yet long life with Me for the obedient. Choose ye this day, October 20, 2020, whom you will serve! If Baal then Baal; if Me, then Me.

The mouth of the Lord is speaking. Can you hear Me now for some didn't hear Me before. I created you; you do know this right? Well, because I created you, if I chose to, **"I can uncreate you."** Some of you don't believe this either.

Those who have an ear, hear this. Revelations 2:17 states, "*He that hath an ear, let him hear what the Spirit saith unto the churches; To him that overcometh will I give to eat of the hidden manna, and will give him a white stone, and in the stone a new name written, which no man knoweth saving he that receiveth it."*

The mouth of the Lord has spoken. Are you *the wheat or the tare?*

The New World Awakening Vision

After M-U-C-H rest, I turned on the TV and was watching a Starbucks cream commercial, WHEN my eyes BLINKED once. It was *in this blink* that everything formatted below was revealed to me. I received this mystery from Holy Spirit.

There is a **New World Awakening**. Spiritual insights and revelations are being born around the world. In the blink of an eye, spiritual downloads come to *the remnant!* Once your eyes blink, especially when the body is rested, each blink...each blink will give an awakening disclosure. Keep blinking for a new adventure in the Spirit. These awakenings are Holy Ghost given. Live for new revelations...anticipate NEW insights, even worldly knowledge to instruct others on how to live. Why? Because you still live on this earth! YOU ARE STILL IN THE WORLD, BUT NOT A PART OF THIS WORLD! You are the transformed spiritual beings about to occupy and take over territories for My glory! You are multiplying, endowed, and being sent out by Yahweh. Fully equipped you are in these transformed bodies.

Because of this spiritual activation, things and people in our midst will become alive and activated. Some will know this and some won't. Life will come to them/it (places and things). This is best described as *spiritual electricity* to other bodies. This is My doing, saith Holy Spirit! Why then? Because I MUST and I WILL take My rightful place and regain My name upon this earth. I NEVER lost it...just will restore it!

This part is almost a holy *NEW WORLD ORDER*, ordered by Yahweh to walk, to live, and to speak for Him on His earth! You are a part of this holy *New World Awakening*. I MUST be and WILL be known around the earth. I know how to glorify Myself. This new spiritual alertness is rising up! This is My doing, and you count it marvelous. It has begun. My daughter—Paris Miller—experienced this awakening today, January 22, 2020. This is why I, Holy Spirit, am having her document this today.

She is arising in this spiritual alertness. Others will enter this realm of glory! "*In the twinkling of an eye,*" it all begins. ALL MUST amp up their faith to join the elite remnant. If you close your eyes, then blink; you can see into parts of heaven. *Closing your eyes causes you to see; blinking gives relations to manifestations.* The storm is almost gone for some remnants that believe. Believing settles it!

Satan's Lustful Torment

From afar, I saw a female that appeared to be riding a bicycle. As I looked closer, she was actually not on a bicycle, yet it was a young lady on a wire fence. One of her legs was on the left side of the fence and the other leg was on the right side of the fence.

This lady appeared to be young and possibly in her early twenties. She had on a skirt and no underwear. I was allowed to see all this. The top of the fence that she straddled had sharp razor wire on top. Satan continually pushed this young lady up the fence and pulled her back down. As he did this, the top of the wire fence tore into her vagina and ripped her private parts.

I knew that she was used to this torment by him. He roared with laughter as he inflicted this pain on her. She appeared to be in a trancelike state as he did his damage to her. I was told that this was "*Satan's lustful torment!*"

Other than to share this vision with others, I still cringe at the thought of this happening to others.

Repent, men and women, so you won't have to suffer this torment and pain in hell.

Holy Spirit uttered to me in August 2020 to place this scripture at the beginning of every prophetic utterance, so here goes:

> *For I testify to everyone who hears the words of the prophecy of this book: If anyone adds to these things, God will add to him the plagues that are written in this book; and if anyone takes away from the words of the book of this prophecy, God shall take away his part from the Book of Life, from the Holy city, and from the things which are written in this book. (Revelations 22:18–19 NKJV)*

Various Prophetic Utterances from January 2020 to December 2020

January 14, 2020, via Chief Apostle Dr. Paris

God is turning things. He is reversing things. He is turning things around for us and those we have been praying for. Don't expect them to come back and thank you because you were doing what you have been called to do. You have endured; you have had tribulations, but I have brought you through them.

All of a sudden, there was a vision of a silhouette around a certain individual in the midst of us. Holy Spirit explained that the silhouette was covering and protection for her and everyone else in attendance.

He continued to say, "You have endured!" Your covering is here now! Some are humbler than others. I am about to exalt you with more revelations and interpretations of dreams and visions. Some won't have to think about what it means; it will roll off their tongue.

At this time, a greater anointing descended in the sanctuary. Just like this experience, He said there will be more. Some will be high for two days after this encounter.

He asked, "Does anyone desire to see into Me?" He answered Himself with, "Desire granted!" Holy Spirit said, "YOU WILL see into Me!"

March 17, 2020, via Chief Apostle Dr. Paris

God is looking for a people that fear Him enough to obey Him. He is searching for a remnant that He can use. Be faithful to God regardless of who doesn't like it. God is trying to take us someplace. When He raised us up last week, He was raising us up and out, even out of the city of Macon. The people outside Macon believe the God in us whereas most of the locals don't (Mark 6:4).

March 22, 2020, via Chief Apostle Dr. Paris

The atmosphere is so light in here today. There is much peace, promise, hope, and prophecies here; I see prophecies blooming like flowers. They are about to come to pass; they are about to be birthed. Prophecies are being revealed and exposed.

CHIEF APOSTLE PARIS (CAP) asked: What do we do Holy Spirit?

HOLY SPIRIT (HS): Wait on Me. I am the prophecy. I am standing before you now.

CAP. I saw (in a vision) HS standing on stage before and in front of us.

HS. I am about to perform for you on stage and off stage. It's your resting time... Let Me work for you.

CAP. Yes, Lord! Show out for us!

HS. You will no longer be an outcast. You are BIG in power; therefore, BIG in Me, even though you look small. Move to the front. Take your rightful position NOW.

CAP. We will. We are.

CAP (*to Oath of Office Apostolic International Ministries Inc.*). We must practice prophesying, meaning we can petition Holy Spirit. We don't have to wait for Him to come upon us.

CAP. What else should we know today, Holy Spirit?

HS. Know that I haven't forgotten you. Know that I KNOW who you are. Know that you are *special* to Me, and I know when your time of unveiling is...NOT before time.

CAP. Thank you, Holy Spirit.

CAP (*teaching note to congregants*). When a *light atmosphere* enters the room, Holy Spirit wants to speak to us. We must then make ready in silence to hear, see, and possibly document!

HS (*to CAP*). I will increase from Me to you regarding ME. You are about to get My double portion of Me. Look at what's happening to you from Me today. I had to put you on hold because the people didn't receive Me through you. I wanted to, but they didn't believe when I spoke through you.

CAP. Holy Spirit, You held off from *the ones* that did believe because there were those that didn't believe?

HS. Yes... I have My reasons. Some of them would have My word as their word.

CAP. HS, you know us well!

CAP. I then heard "Behind the Iron Curtain," tell them:

Lesson PM Taught regarding Hearing His Voice

1. Be silent
2. Make ready to see
3. Make ready to hear
4. Transcend your mind and Spirit to another realm, by focusing outside of yourself
5. **See** Me (Holy Spirit) speaking to you
6. Write down what I speak, and release it NOW!

CAP. Holy Spirit, we need some clarity and direction. We don't know how to proceed. What should we do now!

HS. Keep seeking Me. Continue to gather for Me. Make Me 100 percent your focus.

CAP. Forgive us, HS.

April 5, 2020, via Chief Apostle Dr. Paris

You all have to get lessons quickly. You can't procrastinate or wait. You have to recall it and study the prophecies I have been giving throughout the years. I am connecting the dots. Yes, I am speaking the same things to My leaders, but some things I am only revealing to you all.

Seek Me now. Return to what I have been trying to tell you. Prophecies are blooming like flowers—coming together to make words. They are coming together like a nucleus. They are forming. They aren't waiting on anyone.

You will remember who spoke the prophecy. You will be your own nation. Wake up! I have placed My anointing on you. Remember the prophecies. They are forming, coming together. When they come together, you will have a message.

CAP. What must we do, Holy Spirit (HS)?
HS. Be ready. Just be ready. I continue to warn you. Some are listening and some are not. Come together for the unveiling of the *Kingdom Nation*.

You are a Kingdom Nation. That's why I had CAP name the Apostolic Releases.

You all are My special daughters. Y'all belong to Me. Kingdom Nation for Kingdom Children. Y'all give Me time—I'm giving y'all time.

I'm bending the curve for y'all.

CAP then saw a vision of an arrow shooting forward. A curve then came into the arrow and looked like a boomerang returning to its origin.

I'm returning things back to you. You thought I forgot. Watch for it. You will know when the return comes because it will be multiplied. I always give you more than you give me.

April 17, 2020, via Chief Apostle Dr. Paris

God's progression cannot be measured. There is no inconsistency in God. He is not revealing His mysteries to everyone. It is hard to be a God seeker and a people pleaser at the same time.

April 21, 2020, via Chief Apostle Dr. Paris

I saw a vision of God's mouth. It sucked some people up from the earth. His mouth gave the appearance of a vacuum cleaner. He said that it's a form of protection. I'm taking some people above the enemy's territory. I'm pulling them up above the enemy's clutches. I saw His mouth, and He said, "I'm using My mouth to get them out." These were a lot of people.

"I will send you back when I get ready," He stated.

He didn't just take us up, but *for that moment*, He repositioned us elsewhere in the land.

May 20, 2020, via Chief Apostle Dr. Paris

In resting, Holy Spirit downloads into us our next. Whatever our next is, only He knows when we need to or should be rejuvenated. Otherwise, we are spewing stale bread, stale rhema, when we can and should have fresh rhema, as in when we rest.

1:05 a.m., same day

He said fasting and simultaneously sowing reaps a bigger harvest; not just a financial harvest, but MANY avenues and streams of reaping.

June 13, 2020, via Chief Apostle Dr. Paris

All of us are at a crossroads. We can no longer be stuck. We cannot make ungodly decisions because of friendships or because of love. We are at our crossroad. We have to make godly choices! We have chosen to hold onto friendships rather than follow God.

Unless you are sent by Me, some places we can't visit anymore. When we do, we track mess and poison out of that place into good places. Be mindful of where your feet tread.

We are in a place where we must use wisdom in our fellowships. Everyone is not who they say they are or who they appear to be. They are imitators!

The kingdom is being built differently now. God is raising up the underdogs. He is moving people who are in the way out of the way. He is bringing hunger and thirst back into the household of faith. He has a new crowd, a new team of children. He is redressing us and His ministries for His glory!

Get ready. We can't prepare well enough for what God is doing.

June 18, 2020, via Chief Apostle Dr. Paris

The rain that's coming down is on the just and the unjust. The raindrops form alphabets; the alphabets become words; then the many words form sentences. The sentences are warnings. I (PM) see BEWARE, SEEK, HELP. The help is there that we need. We are in this together.

You can't withhold from the people what God is telling you. The circumference won't be whole without your piece.

Value everything God says to you. God has entrusted us with His promise—in our heart, spirit, and mind. Do you believe it? He has entrusted His promise to all of us. Are we not promise keepers? Let the promise that He has promised you grow. You don't want death of the Spirit.

June 22, 2020, via Chief Apostle Dr. Paris

Holy Spirit spoke to me regarding olHolThe **Doubt Portions (or Blessings)**. He uttered,

- 100 percent portions for those who *don't doubt*
- 80 percent portions for those who *slightly doubt*
- 50 percent portions for those who *frequently doubt*
- 20 percent portions for those who *doubt most of the time*

I will show them, the doubters, again that I AM that I AM. I can penetrate their walls of doubt; however, I want them to trust Me willingly. My 100 percent children, cast this spirit of doubt out of My kingdom. Most haven't received because they doubted. That's why I gave **the percentages of blessings**. Those at 100 percent faith, I have you covered, so that doubt cannot creep in. Your portion is your portion. Stay right there! I have sealed you. What say ye, people of God?

July 2, 2020, via Chief Apostle Dr. Paris

Vision 1 by CAP: God was shuffling and moving people around like a game of chess and checkers. He was jumping people over other people. Why? Because some people were stagnant and they weren't making any progress for Him. They were just there, no movement backward or forward. So the hand of God begins to move those behind the stagnant ones forward by jumping over them or sliding others around them. People were being advanced from the rear quickly. "I'm repositioning and readjusting people around," He said.

Vision 2: Then there was a city. In this city were holy and righteous people; the lips of God blew on the entire city. In doing so, He cleaned the entire city so that the cleansed people of God could continue to inhabit without interruption.

Holy Spirit: You can't prepare well enough for My ascending shifting. Stay in place. Some people won't be shifted but will remain where they are. Expect to see people missing from where they used to be. Don't feel bad when I tell you to go. When I tell you to go—go! I have a purpose and a reason for the shifting. I have to get My people in a place to reach those on the wide road. Stop being closed-mouthed. I use *your voice* to reach a certain kind of people that talk like you. Don't think the words you use can't be used by Me. I gave them to you! Don't get caught with your work undone.

July 5, 2020, via *Chief Apostle Dr. Paris*

The rotation has begun. God has started the shift. Know and do what God has called you to do. God is skipping over those who are not doing anything. He is leaving people where they are. He is not plucking you up—YET. Don't stay in a place where you are not being used.

August 4, 2020, via *Chief Apostle Dr. Paris*

Strange things, as you call them, are about to happen. I am repositioning and realigning people, places, and things. Some people you won't see anymore because you are being repositioned elsewhere. Don't fight against or reject My will for you. **Most** have been trained and are ready for their next, you will see! Go where I send you! All won't be fully 100 percent ready but will still go half-prepared. Why? Because they didn't learn all the lessons as they were given—only a few.

Their interest wasn't in it at the time it was being taught. Why didn't you listen? Why didn't you pay attention and take notes? There are those of you whose fault is not your own. (HS uttered to me that this is because He sent you there, but your leader was disobedient and didn't teach you.) These people will advance forward fully equipped anyway due to *no fault* of their own!

August 6, 2020, via *Chief Apostle Dr. Paris*

We are coming out of one cocoon to another world. They are fighting against God Jehovah. Apostles are pathfinders for the New World Order. We are treaders on paths for others to tread. The unlikely is coming along with us.

August 22, 2020, via Chief Apostle Dr. Paris

Somebody is about to be an eyewitness to an experience—like Jesus was in the temple and turned over the table. Someone is about to be in a place where there is so much chaos. A chosen person will demand order. Don't say, "This is not my house." It's God's house.

Don't just be out of place. Don't be displaced. Some people will never get everything because of being displaced. They think what they're getting is enough, not realizing what God has for them is so much more.

August 25, 2020, via Chief Apostle Dr. Paris

I asked the question on the prayer line, "How many pastors are on the prayer line?"

Holy Spirit said, "Revamp your order in My house. Invite Me back in, and follow Me. I have anointed you to speak for Me and not for man. I am opening My door again for I am switching up and out. I will have order if you don't."

September 18, 2020, via Chief Apostle Dr. Paris

God is about to take us on some journeys, some visitations. This is what He is calling us to do in this season. Next season, we'll be somewhere else.

Holy Spirit is taking us to a place that He has set aside for a specific purpose. A set time, a set place, for a set people; even for a set of people who are ready to be ministered to. I saw a team traveling in the Spirit on a cloud, a platform if you will, going from one place to another—preparing the people in that place to be laborers to go into the harvest.

If you're not ready to go, don't play with God and don't play with His people for there are some big bad demons out there ready to devour. God says you're ready. What He has placed on the inside of us is what is needed for the people.

October 8, 2020, via Chief Apostle Dr. Paris

Be whole and made new; God Jehovah has great plans for us. He provides for us *each other*. There was a vision—I saw the spirit of God pouring water into what looked like an old well. He interpreted this to mean He is priming us for this new awakening. It doesn't matter where we are, what city, or what state we are in. He said, **"What we need is in each other!"** This is why the enemy tries to keep us divided.

What are we doing with the promise inside ourselves? If we can't believe the promise from *the Promise Keeper* given inside ourselves, how will we believe the promise inside of someone else?

October 9, 2020, 5:20 p.m., via Chief Apostle Dr. Paris

There is about to be a weeping spirit throughout the land. There will be a reason to weep. Get right with God so that you won't have a reason to mourn. Repent quickly! We won't be able to rescue some when they start going through their devastation. They heard the same warnings as everyone else. Yes, we will hurt for them, but we can't mourn long. They had the same opportunity that everyone else had.

Then I began to pray like, "Make our ears dull from hearing deception and falseness. Help us to heed Your warnings, Father! What do we do? What is our next move? Someone has to hear it. Don't let us get weary. Don't let the people get disgusted at Your truths, Father."

Then *I saw a vision*: I saw war in the Spirit; so much chaos! (This manifested the same night.) It will be sad to see the weeping spirit unfold.

10:00 p.m., same night

There is a shaking that is taking place in the church.

I (CAP) asked, "God, where are Your people? Where are they? Bring them out. Bring out the real ones. We don't want to be the only ones. Bring them out of hiding. Resurrect them!"

Then I saw them coming out of hiding places, out of buildings, out of ministries, etc. Thank You, Jesus!

October 12, 2020, via Chief Apostle Dr. Paris

Holy Spirit said, "I'm defusing the tare and strengthening the wheat. The remnant is about to bring the harvest!"

October 24, 2020, via Chief Apostle Dr. Paris

Things are changing. The ears of the people are now ready to hear us! Yet, it's not us—it's Him! The favor of the Lord is upon us. People who wouldn't hear Him through us before will now hear.

Vision: I saw Him illuminating us with bright light; I knew that this was His favor! Now run and tell that! God is taking us to a new place where they will see Him and accept Him in this new place.

November 10, 2020, via Chief Apostle Dr. Paris

Don't be deceptive. Take out hardened hearts. Take out lies and be real and tell people the truth. In this season in our lives, if you are doing something good or bad, you will be exposed.

November 11, 2020, via Chief Apostle Dr. Paris

It is time for the new placements in the kingdom. Jehovah God is repositioning us in a new place. It is time to be sent out, so we can equip the saints. Some don't like the condition or state that they are in. They are looking for change. Is that you, or are you the change agent? Repent! God wants to reposition us. We are *the NEW church*! Old churches are closed. Humble yourselves before the mighty hand of God.

November 14, 2020, via Chief Apostle Dr. Paris

Holy Spirit said, "If I can call you out of darkness, why can't I call you to ministry?"

November 16, 2020, via Chief Apostle Dr. Paris

The Holy Spirit said, "Things are changing and shifting for the believers. There will be promotions. I am trying to rush things to My real saints."

He continued to say, "When I send you to a place and some things try to harm you, I will not allow it to happen. Why? Because I sent you! Go where I send you."

December 17, 2020, 10:00 a.m.

Jehovah is rearranging the NOW order of His church. I see some saints in the back being shifted and moved to the front. Positions in God's house will be honored. Those in leadership that didn't acknowledge those that I chose are being replaced. The shifted remnant in their new position is being recrowned to a higher calling because of them being behind too long. What the devil held up actually promoted those that supposedly were "left behind."

When intentional cruelty is inflicted upon My ecclesia, My church, I have a way of putting down one and promoting another. Psalm 75:7 (NLT) says, "It is God alone who judges; He decides who will rise and who will fall." My hand was upon the one being demoted, yet they forgot Who promoted them. This is why there is a constant spiritual shifting in My kingdom. You probably heard years ago the church using the word *shifting*. It is true! When saints usurp their spiritual authority, I shift them.

As the *door of another chance* opens and I continually forgive the disobedient leaders and they don't repent and change, I have to make adjustments to My order of service. I shift the order—always have and always will!

As I told you the first of the year, "They forgot their place, and I will forget their portion!" Did you not believe this?

About the Author

Overseer / Chief Apostle Dr. Paris Miller

Chief Apostle Paris Miller—the leader, the legacy, the love, the professional! Born and raised in a small town in Georgia, Paris has always been known as a giver whose kindness surpasses most. A graduate of Fort Valley State University, Georgia Bible College, and Minnesota School of Theology, she has devoted her life to the kingdom of heaven and the people of God. Dr. Paris is the founder of One Voice Apostolic Ministries International Inc., Oath of Office Apostolic International Ministries Inc., Repairers of the Breach Prayer Ministries, Let's Talk-Wednesday, and Feast of Utopia. As well, she is the overseer of Divine Connections Ministries, One Voice–New Generation Ministries International Inc., The Prayer Chapel, and Hidden Treasures in Earthen Vessels Crusade.

Paris Miller, the leader. She has made it her mission to teach, train, lead, guide, and activate men and women into their rightful position in things of the Spirit in the kingdom of God. With the help and guidance of Holy Spirit, Paris gives the people a voice, a platform to learn, and an office to grow and shine. She is a leader who lowers herself so that others can rise.

She teaches people by asking them questions. This provokes them to seek Holy Spirit for insight and clarity for themselves. She ensures that the people do not become dependent on her but are rather dependent upon Holy Spirit for direction and truth. Under her leadership, Dr. Paris makes sure that the sheep know and seek the voice of God.

Chief Apostle Paris, the legacy. Her legacy speaks for itself. She has left her imprint on the lives of every individual God has left to her charge, whether they have remained with her or not. She continues to live to leave a legacy of holiness, righteousness, love, conviction, and truth. She takes advantage of every opportunity to make a spiritual deposit in the lives of others that cannot be depleted or withdrawn. Paris continues to leave a legacy that is rooted in a foundation of faith, love, prayer, seed sowing, and the Word of God.

Paris Miller, the love. Her hugs are unexplainable. The love, care, concern, reassurance, peace, compassion, joy and healing they bring causes one to confess, weep, and return for more. She has a way of making every person feel like he or she is the most important and only person in the room regardless of his or her background or lifestyle. Her love helps her to reach the unreachable and teach the unteachable. The love that Paris shows comes directly from God who uses her as a vessel to heal, restore, repair and rebuild others. This love Dr. Miller shares commands a response. She is a mother to many, a friend to most, and she knows no stranger.

Paris Miller, the professional. She was selected as Teacher of the Year for two consecutive years at the collegiate level. As well, she is a board member for three establishments. Her accomplishments didn't come easy. She has been relentless in her plight for freedom, love, and peace for those that believed in her mission in life to elevate others with potential. She is a very caring and energetic person to everyone in her midst. Her desire is to assist each gifted person in achieving their vision to the point where she steps in and pulls them forward. She also infuses wisdom into those who seek her counsel.

Paris is a sister, a spiritual mom, an overseer, a mentor, a confidant, an author, a chief apostle, and a teacher. She is a pioneer in things of the Holy Spirit and continues to do the work of ministry so others become pioneers as well. She is determined to do the will of God even if she has to do it alone.

CPSIA information can be obtained
at www.ICGtesting.com
Printed in the USA
JSHW020908040522
25545JS00003B/16